NEWPORT (R.I.)
The Delaplaine
2022
Long Weekend Guide

Andrew Delaplaine

Senior Writer **James Cubby**

NEWPORT (R.I.)
The Delaplaine
Long Weekend Guide

TABLE OF CONTENTS

Chapter 1
WHY NEWPORT?

There are two wildly divergent sides to Newport that have always fascinated me.

On the one hand you have the quaint cobblestone streets lined with galleries, shops, cafés, stores filled with artisanally-crafted wares, tacky tourist traps, the port area where you're reminded that this was a place as connected to the sea as any weather-beaten town on the Maine Coast.

And then on the other hand, you have the "cottages," as the wealthy robber barons of the Gilded Age quaintly called their mega-mansions that make this town unique in all the world.

Back before the 1920s, you could walk up Fifth Avenue and see humongous townhouses owned by some the same families that built these summer "cottages" in Newport (most of which were occupied only for one or two months a year). Most of these houses were designed in the over-the-top ornate Beaux-Arts style favored at the time, everything, of course, copied from European styles America's wealthy sought to replicate with so much fervor in the eternal struggle to become "respectable."

In Manhattan, however, only a few of these houses remain. The Frick, for instance, at 70th Street and Fifth Avenue, is my personal favorite. Its interiors remain mostly as Henry Clay Frick left them except that they've been converted into galleries to display his vast art collection. Other New York houses, such as Andrew Carnegie's 64-room mansion built in 1902 on Fifth Avenue and 91st Street, have been repurposed as homes for nonprofit cultural institutions. In the Carnegie case, his house in now the Cooper-Hewitt Museum. (I've always found the house much more interesting than the exhibits mounted by Cooper-Hewitt sometimes daffy curators, but that's another story.)

As I was saying, most of the houses lining Fifth Avenue were torn down only a decade or two after they were raised at such great expense. The real estate on Fifth Avenue just became so expensive that the families (after income taxes were introduced) decided to sell out rather than preserve these gorgeous houses an fine examples of period architecture. The big apartment blocks you see now on Fifth Avenue replaced those houses.

In Newport, however, the houses did not come down and a grand effort to preserve them was made. That's why they're here for you to marvel at today. And don't even think about coming to Newport if you don't make time for 2 or 3 of these wonderful houses.

Newport is home to any number of internationally recognized festivals and fairs, primary among them the Newport Folk Festival and the Newport Jazz Festival. Be sure to check out the schedules so you know what's going on during your Long Weekend visit.

HOTEL

Chapter 2
WHERE TO STAY

ADMIRAL FITZROY INN
398 Thames St, Newport, 866-848-8780
www.admiralfitzroy.com
This premier getaway offers guests deluxe guestrooms in a European-style bed & breakfast. All rooms are decorated with antique sleigh beds and hand-stenciled armoires. Amenities include: free continental breakfast, private phone line, cable TV, small fridge, and free parking. Two-night minimum required most weekends. Conveniently located near local restaurants and shopping.

THE ALMONDY INN
25 Pelham St, Newport, 401-848-7202
www.almondyinn.com
Conveniently located near Bannister's and Bowens
Wharfs on Narragansett Bay, this restored 1890's
Victorian inn features five elegant guestrooms and
suites decorated with period antiques. Amenities
include: Flat screen TV, DVD player, free Wi-Fi,
signature bath amenities, free bottled water and daily
maid service.

ARCHITECT'S INN
2 Sunnyside Pl, Newport, 401-845-2547
www.architectsinn.com
Constructed in 1873, this palatial guesthouse was
originally the private home of George Champlin
Mason, the famous Newport architect. Located on
"Historic Hill", this Victorian mansion offers
beautifully appointed rooms, suites, and studios
decorated in period furnishings. Amenities include:
free breakfast, free Wi-Fi, free parking, and free

breakfast. Massage therapist available. This inn also hosts Murder Mystery Weekends.

CASTLE HILL INN

590 Ocean Dr, Newport, 888-466-1355
www.castlehillinn.com
Located on 40-acre peninsula overlooking the mouth of Narragansett Bay, this restored 1875 mansion offers a variety of luxurious accommodations including a Swiss-style Chalet, Beach houses and cottages with a private beach. Amenities include: free breakfast, free Wi-Fi, and room service.

CLIFFSIDE INN

2 Seaview Ave, Newport, 401-847-1811
www.cliffsideinn.com
Nestled in the center of the historic district, this elegantly restored 1876 Victorian mansion inn offers beautifully designed guest rooms and suites. Conveniently located near local restaurants and shopping districts, this inn offers a beautiful getaway. Amenities include: whirlpool baths, spa showers, grand beds, LCD TVs, DVD players, iPod sound systems, a serene wrap-around porch, free gourmet breakfast, free Wi-Fi, and free parking.

FORTY 1° NORTH

351 Thames St, Newport, 401-846-8018
www.41north.com
This state-of-the-art hotel and marina is one of
Newport's newest waterfront destinations boasting
both restaurants and lounges. The resort hotel offers
excellent accommodations with environmentally
friendly amenities. All 28 guest rooms offer amenities
like: gas fireplace, iPad, LED 40-inch flat-screen TV,
free Wi-Fi, laptop compatible in-room safe, daily
newspapers and desk-integrated media system. The
resort features beautiful views of Newport Harbor and
Thames Street. In-room spa services available. Pet
friendly accommodations available. Valet parking.

GILDED

23 Brinley St, Newport, 401-619-7758
www.gildedhotel.com

NEIGHBORHOOD: Residential/Near Museum of Newport History

Located in a quiet residential neighborhood, this colorful eclectic 17-room boutique hotel (made up of 2 remodeled Victorian houses, one dating to 1850) offers guest rooms that look like they're from the Gilded Age, but have all the modern conveniences. (Only a few rooms have tubs, so be sure to ask for one if you want a tub.) A free breakfast is offered buffet-style every morning. Gilded is about a 15-minute walk to tourist spots on the water like the restaurant Black Pearl and others. Amenities: Complimentary Wi-Fi, iPod docks, smart TVs, iPads and complimentary breakfast. Hotel features: Guest lounge, secluded patio with croquet practice green, and billiards room. Conveniently located walking distance from the Museum of Newport History and 4 miles from the Ocean Drive Historic District. The owners here have a second property in Newport, the **Attwater**.

MARSHALL SLOCUM GUEST HOUSE
29 Kay St, Newport, 401-841-5120
www.marshallslocuminn.com
Repeatedly named by several publications as "Best Rhode Island Bed and Breakfast," this guesthouse continues to welcome satisfied returning guests. All six rooms are decorated with period antiques with amenities that include: Gilchrist and Soames toiletries, free Wi-Fi, free full morning breakfast, and free parking. Conveniently located just a short walk from downtown Newport and waterfront attractions.

NEWPORT BEACH HOTEL & SUITES
1 Wave Ave, Newport, 401-846-0310
www.newportbeachhotelandsuites.com
Formerly the Inn at Newport Beach, this hotel offers
the largest and most luxurious guest rooms in
Newport County. Amenities include: 37 inch LCD
TV with HD DirecTV, HD DVD/CD player, MP3
player, iPod docking station, free Wi-Fi, and gourmet
coffee and teas. Facilities include: indoor pool and
whirlpool, fitness center with spa treatment room and
rooftop hot tub and firepit. Located steps away from
Easton's Beach and near recreation opportunities
(skateboard park, aquarium and carousel). Private
trainers and fitness instructors available. Free parking.
On-site restaurant.

NEWPORT MARRIOTT
25 Americas Cup Ave, Newport, 401-849-1000
www.marriott.com/hotels/travel/pvdlw-newport-
marriott

This Marriott offers first-class accommodations including perks like a full-service spa, an indoor pool, fitness center and on-site restaurant. This hotel offers 312 rooms and 7 suites on 7 floors. Amenities include: free Wi-Fi, daily newspaper delivery (on request), 32" HDTV, and a laptop safe. This is a smoke-free hotel. Conveniently located near beach facilities and sailing and golfing opportunities.

THAMES STREET GUEST HOUSE

15 Thames St (btw Poplar St and Bridge St), Newport, 401-846-8471
www.15thames.com
Originally an 1869 Italianate Victorian home, this Guest House offers luxurious accommodations. Amenities include: free Continental breakfast, Cable

TV, DVD, free Wi-Fi, an LED fireplace and air conditioning. Conveniently located near downtown Newport and waterfront/harbor areas. Two-night minimum stay on weekends.

HOTEL VIKING
One Bellevue Ave, Newport, 401-847-3300
www.hotelviking.com
This historic hotel offers a wonderful combination of old with modern comfort and amenities. Facility includes: Fitness Center, pool, spa, salon, Jacuzzi, and two on-site restaurants. Amenities include: free Wi-Fi, morning coffee in lobby and daily coffee in room, flat screen LCD TV, and gourmet honor baskets. Children's activities. Smoke free hotel.

Chapter 3
WHERE TO EAT

22 BOWEN'S WINE BAR AND GRILL
22 Bowen's Wharf, Newport, 401-841-8884
www.22bowens.com
CUISINE: American (New)/Steakhouse
DRINKS: Full bar
SERVING: Dinner, Lunch & Dinner on Fri – Sun.
PRICE RANGE: $$$

Nautical-themed eatery serving fresh seafood and high-quality steaks. There's plenty of seating outside, but it's better to go upstairs and overlook the wharf area with all the boats—a better view, in my opinion. My Favorites: Rack of Lamb and Yellowfin Tuna, though it's hard to turn up your nose at the 18-oz bone-in Delmonico, and I didn't, because I rarely see that cut. (The streaks here are all Prime, by the way.) There's a great starter here, the Bucatini Carbonara, rich and satisfying, but a small enough portion so you don't ruin what comes after. Popular brunch destination on weekends. (Get the classic Wedge Salad, the bacon is great.)

BAR 'CINO
22 Washington Sq, Newport, 401-619-8201
https://barcino.com/newport/
CUISINE: Italian

DRINKS: Full Bar
SERVING: Lunch/Dinner
PRICE RANGE: $$
Casual neighborhood eatery offering Italian specialties and grilled pizzas. Favorites: Spaghetti Cacio Pepe and Chicken Picatta. Amazing Tiramisu. Outdoor seating available.

BELLE'S CAFE
1 Washington St, Newport, 401-619-5964
www.newportshipyard.com/bellescafe
CUISINE: Cafe
DRINKS: No Booze
SERVING: Breakfast, Lunch
PRICE RANGE: $$
Boasting a reputation as the best place for breakfast in town, this café also offers a great lunch menu. Menu favorites include: Stuffed French Toast (breakfast) and Jamaican Jerk Chicken (lunch). Great daily specials. Guests get a great view of the Newport Bridge and can watch the yachts come in and out.

BENJAMIN'S RESTAURANT AND RAW BAR
254 Thames St, Newport, 401-846-8768
www.benjaminsrawbar.com
CUISINE: Seafood
DRINKS: Full bar
SERVING: Breakfast, Lunch & Dinner
PRICE RANGE: $$
Casual three-level eatery with a seafood focus. Raw bar. My Favorites: Lobster and Prime Rib. Daily happy hour specials.

BINGE BBQ
12 Broadway, Newport, 401-619-3799
https://bingebbqri.com/
CUISINE: BBQ/American (Traditional)
DRINKS: BYOB
SERVING: Lunch, Dinner; Closed Tuesdays
PRICE RANGE: $$

Compact counter-serve eatery featuring BBQ dishes, sandwiches, and Southern-inspired sides. Favorites: Brisket and Ribs. No Mac & Cheese but they have "Mac and Cheese Croquettes" (Fried Mac and Cheese balls).

BLACK PEARL

Bannister's Wharf, Newport, 401-846-5264
https://www.blackpearlnewport.com/
CUISINE: American/Seafood
DRINKS:
SERVING: Lunch, Dinner, Brunch
PRICE RANGE: $$
Nautical-inspired restaurant with a wharf bar where you can sit, as I have numerous times, and gaze out at the boats docked in front of you. Inside, it's a little

more formal, with white tablecloths. Favorites:
Lobster Benedict and Clams Casino. Chowder is a
must-have. Patio dining in the summer.

BORU NOODLE BAR

36 Broadway, Newport, 401-846-4200
http://www.borunoodlebar.com/
CUISINE: Japanese/Noodles
DRINKS: No Booze
SERVING: Lunch, Dinner; Closed Mondays
PRICE RANGE: $$
Small unprepossessing contemporary eatery with no
frills known locally for their ramen bowls. Favorites:
Pork buns and New England seafood ramen special.
Vegetarian/Vegan options.

BOUCHARD
505 Thames St, Newport, 401-846-0123
https://bouchardnewport.com/
CUISINE: French/International
DRINKS: Full Bar
SERVING: Dinner; Closed Tuesdays

PRICE RANGE: $$$$

Upscale French eatery set in a 1785 Georgian-style
house. Perfect for an elegant dining experience.
Favorites: Dover sole and Twice-stuffed lobster with
scallops. Grand Mariner Souffle is top notch.
Extensive wine list. French martini is amazing.

BRICK ALLEY PUB

140 Thames St, Newport, 401 849-6334
www.brickalley.com
CUISINE: American
DRINKS: Full Bar
SERVING: Lunch, Dinner
PRICE RANGE: $$

Here you'll find a comfortable place to dine plus a
great menu of "pub style" comfort food, steaks, pizza,
pasta, and local seafood. The wine list includes over
250 vintages.
Menu My Favorites: Buffalo Chicken pizza and
Lemony Chicken Piccata. The bar serves an
impressive variety of creative cocktails like the
Chocolate Mint Cookie, a sweet cocktail with a
punch. Gluten-free menu available.

BUSKERS IRISH PUB

178 Thames St, Newport, 401-846-5856
www.buskerspub.com
CUISINE: Irish
DRINKS: Full Bar
SERVING: Breakfast, Brunch, Late night
PRICE RANGE: $$
This old world style pub is decorated with Irish
antiques and features live music on weekends. No

longer serving just "pub" food, this place now boasts to be Newport's only gastropub. Menu favorites include: Filet Mignon wrapped in Irish bacon and Goat Cheese & Prosciutto Shrimp.

CLARKE COOKE HOUSE

24 Bannisters Wharf, Newport, 401-849-2900
www.bannistersnewport.com
CUISINE: Seafood, Sushi Bar
DRINKS: Full Bar
SERVING: Lunch, Dinner
PRICE RANGE: $$$
Located in an 18th century building, the Clarke Cooke House offers several dining options. The Porch, an elegant dining room, The Candy Store, a more relaxed dining situation located at harbor level. Intimate cocktails are available at The SkyBar. Menu favorites include: Summer Sushi. The wine list includes over 400 selections, including everything from regional wines to vintage Bordeaux.

CORNER CAFÉ

110 Broadway, Newport, 401-846-0606
www.cornercafenewport.com
CUISINE: Breakfast/Pizza
DRINKS: No Booze
SERVING: Breakfast & Lunch
PRICE RANGE: $$
Popular locals' breakfast café. My Favorites:
Portuguese sweetbread French toast and Florentine
Eggs Benedict. Tasty wood-grilled pizza. BYOB.

CRU CAFÉ

1 Casino Ter, Newport, 401-314-0500
www.crucafenewport.com
CUISINE: Café/Sandwiches
DRINKS: BYOB
SERVING: 8 a.m. – 5 p.m.
PRICE RANGE: $$
Small café with an outside patio. Order from the
blackboards on the wall behind the counter. Menu
includes breakfast and classic comfort food dishes,

and the menu changes seasonally. My Favorites: Irish
Burrito; a BLT that will knock your socks off, with 2
eggs, smoked bacon, avocado, on a Portuguese roll;
and Poached eggs with avocado toast. BYOB.
(There's a liquor store across the street called Vickers
where you can get a bottle of whatever strikes your
fancy & they'll serve it to you here.)

EMPIRE TEA & COFFEE
22 Broadway, Newport, 401-619-1388
https://empireteaandcoffee.com/
CUISINE: Quick bites/Coffee & Tea
DRINKS: No Booze
SERVING: Breakfast, Lunch, Brunch
PRICE RANGE: $$
Quality coffee and tea emporium offering an
impressive selection of over 70 loose teas. Coffee
comes from local roasters. Their signature drink
selection includes Horchata Chai (hot or frozen) and a

house recipe of spicy hot chocolate. Pastries are plentiful and unique like the chocolate chip donut.

THE DECK

1 Waite's Wharf, Newport, 401-846-3600
www.waiteswharf.com
CUISINE: American/Seafood
DRINKS: Full Bar
SERVING: Lunch, Dinner
PRICE RANGE: $$$
This dockside venue offers fine dining, live entertainment, dancing and an outdoor lounge. Menu favorites include: Pan Seared Sea Scallops and Braised Lamb Shank. Great place for seafood lovers and a nightspot for the 20-30 year old crowd.

DIEGO'S MEXICAN RESTAURANT

11 Bowens Wharf, Newport, 401-619-2640
www.diegosnewport.com

CUISINE: Mexican
DRINKS: Full Bar
SERVING: Lunch, Dinner
PRICE RANGE: $$
This casual eatery offers Mexican cuisine with a modern twist. Menu favorites include: Crispy Pork Belly Tacos and Enchilada del Dia (stuffed enchiladas of the day). Try their creative cocktails like the Passion of Spice (El Buho Mezcal, fresh passion fruit puree, Habanero infused tequila, sour and pineapple juice). Gluten-free menu available.

THE DINING ROOM AT CASTLE HILL INN
590 Ocean Ave, Newport, 401-849-3800
www.castlehillinn.com
CUISINE: American (Traditional)
DRINKS: Full bar
SERVING: Dinner
PRICE RANGE: $$$
Located in the hotel, this beautiful upscale eatery offers several prix fixe menu choices. My Favorites: Yakitori Pork & Beef duo and Seared Yellowfin Tuna. Great views. Impressive wine list. Wine pairings. Very elegant eatery for a special occasion.

Sign outside Flo's

FLO'S CLAM SHACK
4 Wave Ave, Middletown, 401-847-8141
www.flosclamshacks.com
CUISINE: Seafood
DRINKS: Beer & Wine
SERVING: Lunch & Dinner
PRICE RANGE: $$
Right across the Easton Pond in Middleton is this
great place located in an old two-level beach cottage
that survived the hurricane of 1938. Like me, you've

seen a lot of "nautical-themed" restaurants when you travel, and you can tell not a lot of thought went into decorating these places. But Flo's is literally crammed with cast off seafaring items, the walls plastered with everything from oars to life vests to buoys to various signs. It's fun just to walk into the place. There have been several Flo's Clam shacks over the years, but they keep getting destroyed by the many hurricanes that have battered Newport. They always bounce back. The business has been around since the 1930s, and the New England seafood they offer is great. There's a big raw bar upstairs, which is where I like to hang out. My Favorites: White clam chowder and Fish & Chips. Fried Clams is their specialty. You never tasted better.

Outside Flo's (above)

FLUKE WINE BAR & KITCHEN

41 Bowen's Wharf, Newport, 401-849-7778
www.flukenewport.com
CUISINE: American
DRINKS: Full Bar
SERVING: Dinner
PRICE RANGE: $$
This casual two-level eatery located on the water offers a fresh creative seasonal menu. Menu favorites include: Roasted Eggplant Puree and Duck Empanaditas. The bar serves creative cocktails and a nice selection of wines.

FIFTH ELEMENT

111 Broadway, Newport, 401-619-2552
www.thefifthri.com
CUISINE: American
DRINKS: Full Bar
SERVING: Dinner

PRICE RANGE: $$

This combination bar and restaurant offers a great dining experience in a casual atmosphere. The cocktail and martini menu is pretty impressive and the food menu is just as creative. Menu favorites include: Spinach Balls and Lamb Kebob Salad.

FRANKLIN SPA

229 Spring St, Newport, 401-847-3540
No Website
CUISINE: American
DRINKS: No Booze
SERVING: Breakfast, Lunch
PRICE RANGE: $$ / **Cash only**

This down-to-earth diner is a breakfast favorite. Open since 1999, this place serves breakfast all day and great lunch selections. Menu favorites include:

Lobster omelette and Shared Eggs Benedict. Always busy. Cash only.

JO'S AMERICAN BISTRO

24 Memorial Blvd W, Newport, 401-847-5506
www.josamericanbistro.com
CUISINE: American (New)/Seafood
DRINKS: Full bar
SERVING: Dinner nightly, with Lunch added on weekends
PRICE RANGE: $$
Nice cozy little spot popular with locals serving American fare and seafood. My Favorites: Onion jam burger; Duck & Lobster quesadilla; and Lobster carbonara. Creative cocktails like Caramel apple martinis.

LUCIA ITALIAN RESTAURANT

186B Thames St, Newport, 401-846-4477
www.luciarestaurant.com
CUISINE: Italian
DRINKS: Beer & Wine
SERVING: Lunch & Dinner, Dinner only on Mon &
Tues; Closed on Wednesdays
PRICE RANGE: $$
Cute little place in an old brick building with
authentic Northern Italian cuisine offering classic
dishes as well as vegetarian and Gluten-free options.
You definitely want to focus on the pasta dishes here,
because they're about the best you can get in
Newport. My Favorites: Pappardelle alla Carbonara
with Chicken; Manicotti ether with 4 cheeses or with
their delicious homemade Bolognese ragu.

MALT

150 Broadway, Newport, 401-619-1667
No Website
CUISINE: American (New)
DRINKS: Full bar
SERVING: Lunch & Dinner
PRICE RANGE: $$
Cozy little Pub/tavern offering a menu of New
American fare. My Menu picks: Fish & Chips and
Pan Roasted Cod. Great burgers. Delicious desserts.

More than 30 beers on tap with an impressive selection of specialty cocktails.

MAMMA LUISA RESTAURANT
673 Thames St, Newport, 401-848-5257
www.mammaluisa.com
CUISINE: Italian
DRINKS: Beer & Wine
SERVING: Dinner; closed Wednesday
PRICE RANGE: $$
Longtime favorite serving classic Italian fare. Their Gnocchi can't be beat. Monday & Tuesday night specials. Nice selection of wines – mostly from the region.

MIDTOWN OYSTER BAR
345 Thames St, Newport, 401-619-4100
www.midtownoyster.com
CUISINE: American
DRINKS: Full Bar
SERVING: Lunch, Dinner
PRICE RANGE: $$
This is a top-notch seafood multi-level restaurant with the largest raw bar in Newport. Menu favorites include: Caramelized Sea Scallops and Oven Roasted Twin Lobster Tails. First floor has live music. Very busy.

MOORING SEAFOOD KITCHEN & BAR

1 Sayer's Wharf, Newport, 401-846-2260
www.mooringrestaurant.com
CUISINE: Seafood
DRINKS: Full Bar
SERVING: Breakfast, Lunch, Dinner
PRICE RANGE: $$$
This charming seafood eatery offers an amazing
dining experience featuring indoor and outdoor
dining. Their wine list features many of New
England's best and includes more than 600 labels.
Menu favorites include: Croissant Lobster Roll and
Portuguese Roasted Cod. Gluten-free menu available.
Reservations recommended.

PERRO SALADO

19 Charles St, Newport, 401-619-4777
www.perrosalado.com
CUISINE: Mexican

DRINKS: Full Bar
SERVING: Dinner, Lunch on Sun
PRICE RANGE: $$
This place serves great creative traditional Mexican fare. The portions are large and you won't be disappointed. Menu favorites include: Mexican Scallops and Sticky Ribs. Great margaritas and sangria. Reservations recommended.

POUR JUDGEMENT

32 Broadway, Newport, 401-619-2115
www.pourjudgementnewport.com
CUISINE: American
DRINKS: Full Bar
SERVING: Lunch, Dinner
PRICE RANGE: $$
Popular restaurant among locals, this place offers a creative menu featuring soups, salads, sandwiches, seafood, and pastas. Nice selection of craft beers. Menu favorites include: Gouda Cheese Fries and Thai Shrimp Curry Nachos.

RED PARROT

348 Thames St, Newport, 401-847-3800
www.redparrotrestaurant.com
CUISINE: American
DRINKS: Full Bar
SERVING: Lunch, Dinner
PRICE RANGE: $$

One of the city's most popular restaurants, this eatery offers an eclectic 20-page menu prepared in two separate kitchens. Located in a historic building, there are three floors of dining and four bars. Menu favorites include: Blackened Mahi Mahi and Mandarin Coconut Chicken. Bar menu features assortment of creative cocktails and frozen drinks. Popular for large parties.

RESTAURANT BOUCHARD

505 Thames St, Newport, 401-846-0123

www.bouchardnewport.com
CUISINE: French
DRINKS: Full bar
SERVING: Dinner; closed Tuesday
PRICE RANGE: $$$
Classic French eatery complete with white table cloths and menu in French. My Favorites: Rack of Lamb and Duck breast. Nice wine list. Everything is good here.

SALVATION CAFÉ
140 Broadway, Newport, 401-847-2620
www.salvationcafe.com
CUISINE: Varied
DRINKS: Full bar
SERVING: Dinner
PRICE RANGE: $$
Trendy eatery with a tiki bar outside when the weather's good. The cuisine served here ranges from

Mongolian BBQ baby back ribs to Teriyaki Salmon to Cajun Jambalaya, so it's kind of all over the place. I've been here several times and can attest that everything is carefully prepared and very good. My Favorites: Lemon Herb Brick Chicken; the Short-rib burger. Creative cocktails. Happy hour specials.

SARDELLA'S ITALIAN RESTAURANT
30 Memorial Blvd W, Newport, 401-849-6312
www.sardellas.com
CUISINE: Italian/Pizza
DRINKS: Full bar
SERVING: Dinner
PRICE RANGE: $$
Casual eatery serving up hearty Italian fare. Fresh seafood and a nice variety of pasta dishes. My Favorites: Prosciutto Pizza and the Meatballs. Large restaurant with outdoor seating. Locals' favorite.

SCALES AND SHELLS

527 Thames St, Newport, 401-846-3474
https://www.scalesandshells.com/
CUISINE: Seafood/American
DRINKS: Full Bar
SERVING: Dinner
PRICE RANGE: $$$
This upscale Newport favorite offers a creative menu
of seafood and pastas. Favorites: Mako Shark Steak
and Linguini with clam sauce. Raw Bar. Open-

kitchen. No reservations. Asian inspired dishes.
Impressive cocktail list. Outdoor seating available.

SCARPETTA
GURNEY'S RESORT
1 Goat Island, Newport, 401-849-2600
www.gurneysresorts.com/newport/dining/scarpetta
CUISINE: Italian
DRINKS: Full bar
SERVING: Dinner only 4 nights weekly; Closed Sun,
Mon & Tues.
PRICE RANGE: $$$
Upscale slick, modern hotel eatery offering classic
Italian dishes expertly prepared by the team at
Scarpetta, which now has a half dozen locations
around the country. Very fancy, very nice, but not as
expensive as you might imagine (not at this location,
anyway). My Favorites: Duck & Foie Gras Ravioli
that's sinfully rich and delicious; Seared Diver
Scallops that melt in your mouth and the Loin of

Lamb in an herb crust that bursts with flavors. Creative cocktails. World-class wine list. Patio with a harbor view. There are a couple of other options here at the Gurney Resort, like the **Lounge and Firepit** where you can have a quiet cocktail, or the **Pineapple Club**, which is their outdoor bar overlooking the water. All very nice.

THE WHARF PUB AND RESTAURANT
37 Bowen's Wharf, Newport, 401-619-5672
www.wharfsouthernkitchen.com/
CUISINE: Argentinean
DRINKS: Full Bar
SERVING: Breakfast, Brunch, Late night
PRICE RANGE: $$
Their porch is a popular place to watch the action on Bannister's Wharf however dining inside the cozy dining room is best. The menu of pub food also includes meat, seafood, and pasta entrees. Menu favorites include: Roasted Turkey Meatloaf and BBQ Pork Shoulder Mac N Cheese. There's also a raw bar and a gluten-free menu. The bar offers 28 bottled beers and micro brews and a list of creative cocktails. Live music on Wednesday nights.

WHITE HORSE TAVERN
26 Marlborough St, 401-849-3600
www.whitehorsenewport.com
CUISINE: American
DRINKS: Full Bar
SERVING: Lunch, Dinner
PRICE RANGE: $$$

Built in 1652, this is the oldest bar in the nation. This historic venue offers fine dining in an elegant setting. There are two bars and you must try a Darn and Stormy, the unofficial cocktail of Newport. The Tavern features a contemporary culinary experience with a menu that includes fresh local fish, clams, and lobster. Menu favorites include: Lobster Mac & Cheese and New England Style Crabcake.

ZELDA'S NEWPORT

528 Thames St, Newport, 401-849-4002
https://www.zeldasnewport.com/
CUISINE: American (New)/Seafood
DRINKS: Full Bar
SERVING: Dinner, Brunch on Sundays

PRICE RANGE: $$$
Intimate neighborhood eatery offering
French/American fare with a seafood focus. Menu
picks: Grilled Salmon and Fried Cod. Local bar
atmosphere.

Chapter 4
NIGHTLIFE

BOOM BOOM ROOM
Clark Cook House
26 Bannister's Wharf, Newport, 401-849-2900
www.clarkecooke.com
Located in the basement of Clark Cook House restaurant, this nightspot offers music and dancing. This popular discotheque is very dark and attracts an eclectic crowd of all ages.

THE FASTNET PUB

1 Broadway, Newport, 401-845-9311
www.thefastnetpub.com
This popular local pub offers a variety of beers on
tap, simple but strong cocktails, and a great place to
catch the sports games on TV. Like your old-time
pubs, this place has dartboards, a pool table, and a
back patio for smoking. There's a simple menu of pub
fare like fish and chips. Irish music night every
Sunday.

NEWPORT BLUES CAFÉ

286 Thames St, Newport, 401-841-5510
www.newportblues.com/
Housed in a historic brownstone built in 1892, this
world-class, live music venue offers an impressive
roster of local and national acts with a variety of
music genres represented including classic rock,
blues, progressive, indie rock and hip-hop.

O'BRIEN'S PUB

501 Thames St, Newport, 401-849-6623
www.theobrienspub.net/
Located in the fifth ward district of Newport, this pub
is a local's favorite for its bar scene but also offers a
large menu for lunch and dinner. During summer
season, the outdoor garden patio is quite popular and
a great place to enjoy cocktails or dinner. The bar
offers a variety of video games, pool tables and 5
TVs.

ONE PELHAM EAST
270 Thames St, Newport, 401-847-9460
www.thepelham.com
Open since 1975, this is Newport's oldest rock club.
The place has booked its share of celebrity rock and
reggae performers and has been a favorite hangout for
the America's Cup sailing teams. Live bands and a
dance floor. Open 7 nights a week.

Chapter 5
WHAT TO SEE & DO

ADIRONDACK II

23 Bowens Wharf, Newport, 401-847-0000
www.sail-newport.com
Built in 1999 by Scarano Boat Building, this 80-foot
boat is representational of a classic turn-of-the-
century Pilot Schooner. A cruise aboard the
Adirondack II is an experience as it passes Newport's
stately bayside mansions, a 19th Century military fort
and beautiful old lighthouses. This schooner can
accommodate up to 60 passengers. Prices vary

depending on the type of cruise. Available for corporate and private sailing charters, day sails and sunset cruises.

ANTIQUE YACHT COLLECTION

31 Bowens Wharf, Newport, 401-678-6740
www.antiqueyachtcollection.com
Private boat charter that offers a variety of VIP charter services. Private cruises for groups of six or less. What's really great are these beautiful old yachts exquisitely maintained.

AQUIDNECK GROWERS WEDNESDAY FARMERS MARKET

Memorial Blvd. & Chapel St., Newport, no phone
https://guide.farmfreshri.org/food/farmersmarkets_details.php?market=2
Open every Wednesday (June 4 – October 29, 2 – 6 p.m.) this weekly Farmers Market offers a great marketplace with more than 25 vendors selling both organic and conventionally-grown products including: fresh vegetables, cut flowers, herbs, berries, fruit, plants, eggs, breads, baked goods, meats, seafood, and cheeses. There's also live music.

ARBORETA TOURS

www.newportarboretumweek.org
Tour some of Newport's finest landscapes and tree collections at some of the best private Newport estates that open their grounds for tours.

BRETON POINT STATE PARK

Ocean Drive, Newport, 401-849-4562

www.riparks.com/Locations/LocationBrentonPoint.ht
ml
Occupying the former grounds of one of Newport's
grandest estates, this park offers spectacular views as
it's located at the point where Narragansett Bay meets
the Atlantic Ocean. Visitors can enjoy the view,
picnic, hike, and fish. Open year round. No fees.

BRICK MARKET HISTORIC DISTRICT
221 Goddard Row, Newport
www.brickmarketnewport.com
The Newport Historic District covers 250 acres in the
center of that city with a selection of intact colonial
buildings. The historic buildings include the city's
oldest house and the former meeting place of the
colonial and state legislatures. Set on Newport's
waterfront, this is a favorite tourist attraction.

CLASSIC CRUISES OF NEWPORT
Bannister's Wharf, 401-847-0298
www.cruisenewport.com
Classic Cruises offers a great variety of water
entertainment including sailing, powerboat tours and
sunset cocktail harbor cruises. Cruises feature
spectacular views of Newport Harbor and
Narragansett Bay. Choose from a 72' Schooner or a
high-speed motor yacht. Modest fees depending on
tour.

CLIFF WALK
www.cliffwalk.com
This scenic three and a half mile walkway borders the
back lawn of The Breakers and several other beautiful

Newport Mansions. This is one of the top attractions in Newport. The walk runs from the east end of Bailey's Beach to the west end of First Beach.

FORT ADAMS
90 Fort Adams Dr, Newport, 401-841-0707
www.fortadams.org
This State Park offers panoramic views of Newport Harbor and the East Passage of Narragansett Bay. Park activities include: saltwater bathing, fishing, boating, soccer, rugby, and picnicking. The park is known for its annual summer concerts. Permits needed to play rugby and soccer. Tours available.

**INTERNATIONAL TENNIS HALL OF FAME
AT THE NEWPORT CASINO**
194 Bellevue Ave, Newport, 401-849-3990
www.tennisfame.com
Housed in the historic Newport Casino, this venue
celebrates the history of tennis dating from the 12th
Century to the present. The Hall of Fame has 18
galleries with over 20,000 square feet of interactive
exhibits, videos, and tennis memorabilia. The
collection contains over 16,000 objects. Open daily.
Nominal admission fee.

JANE PICKENS THEATER
49 Touro St, Newport, 401-846-5252
www.janepickens.com
Located in Washington Square, this world-class art
house cinema happens to be one of America's oldest
theaters. The theater offers an impressive schedule of
films, documentaries, and public events.

KRISTEN COATES ART & HOME
152 Bellevue Ave, Newport, 401-684-0211
www.kristencoates.net
Gallery & gift shop on Bowen's Wharf featuring art
and objects for the well curated home including
contemporary art, collectibles and artisan made
objects. Classes available.

**MUSEUM OF NEWPORT
HISTORY/NEWPORT HISTORICAL SOCIETY**
127 Thames St, 401-841-8770
www.newporthistory.org
NEIGHBORHOOD: Historic district

ADMISSION: Free
The Society operates several historical facilities and supports and preserves, through documentation and exhibition, the history of Newport County. The museum, located in the 1762 Brick Market, offers an engaging introduction to Newport's rich history. Acting as an information center, this is also the departure point for guided walking tours. Exhibits include: James Franklin's printing press, photographs, furniture, colonial silver, paintings, and historical objects from the collections of the Newport Historical Society.

THE *M/V GANSETT*, GANSETT CRUISES
2 Bowens Wharf, Newport, 401-787-4438
www.gansettcruises.com
Cruises aboard the M/V Gansett offer a scenic tour of Newport and Jamestown. One and a half hour narrated harbor tours and sunset cruises available. Both cruises offer cocktails, beer and wine. The M/V Gansett is a well-appointed private yacht manned by

well-informed guides. Price varies depending on cruise.

NATIONAL MUSEUM OF AMERICAN ILLUSTRATION

492 Bellevue Ave, Newport, 401-851-8949
www.americanillustration.org
Founded in 1998 by Judy and Laurence S. Cutler to house their art collection, this museum now exhibits art from all periods and styles. The museum building is an interpretation of an 18th century French chateau with three-acre grounds inspire by King Henry VIII's garden. The museum offers one of the greatest collections of American illustrations in perpetuity. Open year-round by advance reservation for group and VIP tours.

NAVAL WAR COLLEGE MUSEUM

686 Cushing Rd, Newport, 401-841-4052
https://www.usnwc.edu/museum
This museum's exhibitions celebrate the history of naval warfare and the naval heritage of Narragansett Bay. The collection museum offers exhibits pertaining to the genesis of the Navy in the region. Open daily. Reservations necessary made one working day in advance. Non-U.S. Citizens require 14 days advance notice.

NEWPORT ART MUSEUM

76 Bellevue Ave, Newport, 401-848-8200
www.newportartmuseum.org
This museum celebrates Newport and Rhode Island's rich cultural heritage. The museum's permanent

collection of over 2,300 works of American art focuses on 19th century to present day featuring artists like Howard Gardiner Cushing, Dale Chihuly, Richard Merking, James Baker, Rita Rogers and Sue McNally.
Nominal admission fee. Closed Mondays.

NEWPORT DISTILLING COMPANY/THOMAS TEW DISTILLERY

Coastal Extreme Brewing Company
293 J. T. Connell Rd, Newport, 401-849-5232
www.newportcraft.com
See firsthand how run is made and taste single barrel rum in the 3 stages of the aging process. The Visitors Center is open everyday (except Tuesdays) for tours and tastings. Visitors can view the distillery from the tour deck or enjoy one of the daily-guided tours (3 p.m.). Reservations not necessary. Nominal admission fee. Group private tours available.

NEWPORT GULLS BASEBALL TEAM

20 Americas Cup Ave, Newport, 401-845-6832
www.newportgulls.com
This is a wooden-bat, summer collegiate baseball team called the Newport Gulls. The team has won several NECBL Championships. Check website for schedule.

NEWPORT HARBOR SHUTTLE

Newport Harbor Dr, Portsmouth, 401-847-9109
www.newportharborshuttle.com
Shuttle tour of the harbor starting at Perrotti Park by the Marriott. This 55-minute round trip tour makes

six stops including Fort Adams. Tour guides are very informative. Minimal fee for the whole day allows you to hop off and get back on at no additional charge.

NEWPORT SHIPYARD

1 Washington St, Newport, 401-846-6000
www.newportshipyard.com
Full service boatyard and marina, ship store, restaurant and fitness center. You'll see some of the biggest superyachts on the East Coast docked here. It's fun to drop in at **Bella's Café** for breakfast or lunch.

NORMAN BIRD SANCTUARY

583 Third Beach Rd, Middletown, 401-846-2577
www.normanbirdsanctuary.org
Established in 1949 at the bequest of Mabel Norman Cerio, this 325-acre sanctuary offers diverse habitats to study birds. Guided bird walks available (every other Sunday beginning at 8 a.m.). Walks are free for members, a nominal fee is charged for non-members.

THE OCEAN DRIVE

www.oceandrivenewport.com
Ocean Drive offers ten miles of historic landmarks and breathtaking views of the Atlantic Ocean. Take RI-138 east or RI-114 south and follow the signs for RI-138A/Memorial Boulevard and turn right on Bellevue Drive heading south and the scenic drive begins.

REDWOOD LIBRARY AND ATHENAEUM
50 Bellevue Avenue, Newport, 401-847-0292
www.redwoodlibrary.org
NEIGHBORHOOD: Historic District
ADMISSION: Minimal Fee; guided tours Saturday at
10:30 a.m. – included with admission.
Founded in 1747, this is the oldest community library
still in the original building in the United States.
Besides beautiful books, the library exhibits
paintings, busts, sculptures, and decorative arts. Two
galleries feature revolving exhibitions.

ROUGH POINT
680 Bellevue Ave, Newport, 401-847-8344
www.newportrestoration.org
This is one of the Gilded Age mansions, formerly the
Newport home of heiress Doris Duke; this beautiful
oceanfront estate is now open as a museum. Still
decorated as the infamous philanthropist and art
collector left it, this mansion is filled with French
furniture, European art, Chinese porcelains, and
Turkish carpets. Tours last about 75 minutes.
Nominal admission fee.

SAMUEL WHITEHORNE HOUSE MUSEUM
416 Thames St, Newport, 401-847-8344
www.newportrestoration.org
This Federal style mansion is open to the public as a
historic house museum. The museum contains some
of the best examples of Newport and Rhode Island
furniture from the late 18th century including
examples of craftsmen from the renowned Townsend

and Goddard workshops. Open Thursday – Monday. Nominal admission fee, guided tours available.

TOURO SYNAGOGUE NATIONAL HISTORIC SITE

85 Touro St, Newport, 401-847-4794
www.tourosynagogue.org
Built in 1763, the Touro Synagogue is the oldest synagogue still standing in the United States and the only surviving synagogue in the U.S. dating back to the colonial era.
Nominal admission fee. Tours available. Closed on Saturdays.

WILLIAM VAREIKA FINE ARTS

212 Bellevue Ave, Newport, 401-849-6149
www.vareikafinearts.com
One of the largest and most respected galleries in the U.S. featuring 18th, 19th and early 20th century works of art, with items from Hudson Valley illuminist painters. Stained glass artist John La Farge is also featured here.

Chapter 6
NEWPORT'S "COTTAGES"

NEWPORT MANSIONS
The Preservation Society of Newport County
www.newportmansions.org
401-847-1000

This is a central website where you can explore some of the houses open to the public and buy tickets good to more than one tour.

If you only have time for 2 or 3 houses, tour the **Breakers**, the **Elms** and **Rough Point**. Those are my 3 favorites.

Also, if you have the time, I urge you to take the **Servants Life Tour** at the Elms. This tour focuses on the lives of the people who staffed these mansions. You'll hear the stories of the butler, Ernest Birch; his wife, cook Grace Rhodes; and one of the maids, Nellie Lynch Regoli. You have to climb up 82 stairs of the back staircase from the basement servant entrance to the third floor staff quarters, where you'll see exhibits and pictures of the people who lived and worked here. You even get to go out onto the roof where you'll get a stunning view of the estate and Newport Harbor beyond. The second part of the tour takes you back down the 82 steps where you'll see the basement kitchens, coal cellar, boiler room and laundry rooms.

Houses covered on the web site are:

THE BREAKERS

Cornelius Vanderbilt II, grandson to Commodore Vanderbilt, the family patriarch, built this house in 1893, and it's still the biggest of all the "cottages" in Newport.

MARBLE HOUSE
This is another Vanderbilt property, built by William
K. Vanderbilt, to be exact.

THE ELMS

Built for Edward Berwind (a coal magnate from Philadelphia) and finished in 1901, this is a beautiful house modeled on the Chateau d'Asnieres on the outskirts of Paris. This is the house offering tours of the servants' quarters I mentioned above.

ROSECLIFF

Famed architect Stanford White (yes, the guy who got shot in the head at Madison Square Garden by his mistress's jilted lover) got the commission to built this house for Tessie Oelrichs, who inherited her money from her daddy, James Fair, who made it in the Nevada silver mines. (She was born in Virginia City, NV). The history of these Newport houses is also the history of the self-made billionaires of the Gilded Age, and there are dozens of colorful life stories involved. White used the Grand Trianon (a garden getaway at Versailles where French kings relaxed) as his inspiration for this house.

CHATEAU-SUR-MER

This is one of the older houses, dating back to 1852, and was perhaps the grandest until the Vanderbilts started erecting houses in the 1890s. The house was built by William Wetmore, who made his money on the Yankee clippers that traded between the U.S. and China. Architect Richard Morris Hunt (the pre-eminent architect of the Gilded Age who went on to oversee construction of many houses in Newport and along Fifth Avenue) designed the house using influences from the French Second Empire.

KINGSCOTE

Dating back to 1839, Kingscote is the best example you're likely to find in the Gothic Revival style. Sure,

many towns have examples of this type of
architecture, but they weren't built with the kind of
money a Newport owner could throw at the project. It
was built by a Southern planter, George Noble, but
his family never returned to Newport after the Civil
War broke out, and it passed into the hands of
William King, another guy who made his fortune in
the China trade. In the 1870s, the place was given a
makeover by the distinguished firm of McKim, Mead
& White (as in the aforementioned Stanford White).
Some of Louis Comfort Tiffany's earliest work can
be seen here in the translucent colored "bricks" he
used.

Other houses covered are: **ISAAC BELL HOUSE,
GREEN ANIMALS TOPIARY GARDEN, the
HUNTER HOUSE** and **CHEPSTOWE.**

Other notable great houses in Newport not covered by
the website above:

ASTOR BEECHWOOD MANSION

http://www.newport-discovery-guide.com/beechwood-mansion.html

This was the Astor family's summer getaway place, now privately owned by a software billionaire and not open to the public.

BELCOURT CASTLE

http://www.belcourt.com/

Once owned by a Belmont, this house is in private hands once again.

OCHRE COURT

http://www.newport-discovery-guide.com/newport-mansions-ochre-court.html

This grand house (only the Vanderbilts' Breakers is bigger) is a little off the radar because it's owned by

the school, the Religious Sisters of Mercy.
Descendants of the rich banker who built it in 1892
gave it to the church in 1947. You can go onto the
grounds anytime you want and even have a look
inside the house, where you'll be surprised at the
grandness of the interior design.

ROUGH POINT
Newport Restoration Foundation
www.newportrestoration.org
This foundation was set up by Doris Duke, and it
manages **Rough Point,** her oceanfront mansion here.
This is definitely a worthy stop on your visit. Duke
was the heiress, philanthropist and art collector.
Enjoy her magnificent oceanfront estate, still
decorated as she left it, where you will see French
furniture, European art, Chinese porcelains, and
Turkish carpets collected from exotic locations
around the world. Located on Newport's exclusive
Bellevue Avenue, Rough Point provides a sweeping

ocean view and expansive grounds designed by renowned landscape architect Frederick Law Olmsted, whose other little project in his life was designing Central Park in New York.

OCHRE COURT
(below)

Chapter 7
SHOPPING & SERVICES

BRAHMIN LEATHER WORKS
22 Bannister's Wharf, Newport, 401-849-5990
www.brahmin.com
This shop sells the handcrafted Brahmin handbag that is both elegant and long lasting. The brand is known worldwide. Here you'll find handbags and accessories.

COOKIE JAR
29 Bowen's Wharf, Newport, 401-846-5078
https://bowenswharf.com/directory/the-cookie-jar/
Since 1977, this little bakery has been selling sweets to locals and visitors. Here you'll find an assortment of fresh muffins, scones, cinnamon rolls, cookies, breakfast sandwiches, bagels, and banana bread. Of course many come for the vast variety of cookies baked fresh daily.

NEWPORT SUNGLASS SHOP
BRICK MARKET PLACE
109 Swinburne Row, Newport, 401-846-6444

https://newportsunglass.com/
This eyewear boutique is known as Newport's experts in sunglasses and eyewear. Hottest designer frames available like Smith Optics, Ray-Ban's, Oakley, and Maui Jim.

NEWPORT WINE CELLAR

5 Merton Rd, Newport, 401-619-3966
www.newportwinecellar.com
Since 2008, this unique shop offers a great selection of high quality, small production wines from all wine producing regions. Weekly wine tastings and seminars are offered. Occasional offerings of craft beers.

PINK PINEAPPLE

380 Thames Rd, Newport, 401-849-8181
www.pinkpineappleshop.com
This boutique offers the Pink Pineapple cashmere collection designed by Stacie Hall. Here you'll find a

beautiful selection of luxurious cashmere fashions as well as accessories, bracelets, and earrings.

PLEASANT SURPRISE
Brick Market Place

121 Swinburne Row, Newport, 401-846-1202
www.pleasant-surprise.com **WEBSITE DOWN AT PRESSTIME**

Aptly named, this shop offers an eclectic mix of gifts, books, cards, toys, and home accessories. Most gift items have a nostalgic theme. Perfect place to buy a fun gift.

Shipping available.

TEN SPEED SPOKES
18 Elm St, Newport, 401-847-5609
www.tenspeedspokes.com

For more than 40 years this shop has been selling and servicing bicycles. This is a full-service bicycle shop that offers women's and men's clothing, shoes, sunglasses and accessories. Bicycle rentals available.

INDEX

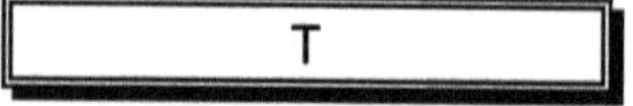

TEN SPEED SPOKES, 83
**THAMES STREET GUEST
HOUSE**, 16
TOURO SYNAGOGUE, 70

WHARF PUB, 49

WHITE HORSE TAVERN,
49
**WILLIAM VAREIKA FINE
ARTS**, 70

Z

ZELDA'S NEWPORT, 50